Original title:
Lemon Blossoms in the Air

Copyright © 2025 Creative Arts Management OÜ
All rights reserved.

Author: Derek Caldwell
ISBN HARDBACK: 978-1-80586-427-1
ISBN PAPERBACK: 978-1-80586-899-6

Blossoming in Radiant Yellows

In a garden where sunshine plays,
Petals giggle in warm, bright rays.
Buzzing bees dance on sweet, fresh air,
Wearing yellow hats, oh, look at their flair!

Sprightly scents tickle our nose,
While goofy squirrels strike silly poses.
Each bloom sways, with laughter rife,
In this whimsical wonder we call life.

In the Shadow of Citrus Trees

Underneath the leafy shade,
A lemon's grin is perfectly made.
Branches whisper, 'Let's play a game!'
As we chase shadows, none are the same!

A rogue breeze stirs the scene with glee,
Knocking hats off, oh, woe is me!
Citrus giggles, mingling bright,
Turning the garden into pure delight.

The Joy of Sun-Drenched Florals

Sunny blooms wear a jaunty air,
In their cheerful jackets, they wholeheartedly dare.
They tease the wind and spark a chase,
Flirting with bees in a lighthearted race!

Petals wobble with such great zest,
Challenging the sun to a wacky test.
Sunshine laughter fills the breeze,
Nature's own party, oh, if you please!

Echoes of Citrus Delights

In the orchard of giggles and cheer,
Echoes of laughter draw us near.
A fruit's bright yellows spark joy anew,
Even the crows dance; can you see them too?

Fruity aromas tickle the brain,
While children chase, calling out in vain.
Through the joy of zestful romps,
Nature's laughter in every stomp!

Essence of the Sunlit Grove

In the grove, the bees do dance,
Their buzzing song, a merry prance.
An orange cat in sunlit spots,
Chases his tail, but ties in knots.

A squirrel swings, with nuts in tow,
He wears a hat, oh what a show!
The trees are laughing, leaves agree,
Nature's court jester, wild and free.

Nectar in the Morning Dew

A honey jar sits by my feet,
Inviting ants for a sweet feast.
They march like soldiers, neat and proud,
In search of goodies, quite allowed.

A wind-up frog leaps in the grass,
Giggling frogs, oh how they pass!
Kites fly high with silly cheer,
Chasing rainbows, no hint of fear.

The Scent of Forthcoming Sunshine

A quirky crow with a shiny cap,
Sips from puddles, takes a nap.
He dreams of fields and flocks of cheer,
While dandelions whisper near.

The sun peeks out, a shy display,
Making shadows dance and sway.
Poor socks, there's not a pair in sight,
Washed away in the wild delight.

Bright Petals Against Blue Skies

Pigeons strut with such great flair,
In their tuxedos, debonair.
They gossip 'bout the best seed spots,
Like tiny suits with little thoughts.

A butterfly joins the fashion show,
Spreading wings, oh what a glow!
The daisies laugh, they spin around,
In this wild garden, joy is found.

A Festival of Fragrant Petals

In the garden, bees do dance,
Wearing yellow pants, what a chance!
The flowers giggle, tickling the nose,
While butterflies prance in fancy clothes.

Smells like lemonade, oh what a treat,
With every step, there's joy in defeat.
The sun winks down, sharing a joke,
As squirrels crack nuts, puffing on smoke.

Dappled Light on Citrus Dews

Underneath a shady tree,
Lemons plot their spree, oh wee!
The dappled light plays tag with the breeze,
While ants conspire 'round biscuits and cheese.

A citrus sunbeam, bright and bold,
Gives goofy grins to all the old.
And laughter erupts from green leaves so spry,
As rabbits hop in their jolly tie-dye.

Treasure of the Orchard's Heart

In the orchard, pirates roam,
With capes made of fruit, they find their home.
A treasure map drawn on a lemon slice,
They dig for giggles, oh how nice!

With every scoop, more laughter flows,
As splashes land on the pig in prose.
The sun sets low, painting the sky,
While cherries cheer, oh me, oh my!

Sun's Hand on Delicate Blooms

The sun gives a high five to every bud,
While flowers blush in a bright green flood.
Dancing shadows leap on the ground,
Crickets sing silly, a lively sound.

As the day moves on, smiles abound,
Fruits tossing jokes, all around.
A playful breeze steals the show,
With soft whispers of where to go!

Scented Echoes of Dawn

Awake with the scent of bright sun's glee,
A buzzing bee sings, 'Come dance with me!'
The flowers giggle, they can't keep still,
While frogs fashion hats from the nearby hill.

With each gust of laughter, petals will sway,
While dogs chase their tails in the morning spray.
A cat makes a fuss and jumps in the fray,
Who knew dawn's perfume could lead to ballet?

Dance of the Yellow Petals

Atop a hill, the petals do shimmy,
As squirrels jive with moves oh so skimmy!
A breeze tickles noses, oh what a tease,
While birds sport pink tutus and preen with ease.

They twirl and spin, in a floral rave,
While bumblebees boast of the honey they save.
The daisies shout, 'We've got some flair!'
With pollen confetti that drifts through the air!

Floral Serenade in the Wind

A bouquet of voices in the garden sings,
A chorus of critters on bright, flowery wings.
The daisies are crooning, a soft, silly tune,
As rabbits perform under a rosy-hued moon.

With dandelions blowing their wishes around,
The frogs lead the charge with a leap and a bound.
A weathered old gnome joins the merry crew,
Proclaiming tomorrow he'll paint himself blue!

Citrus Kisses at Twilight

Twilight brings giggles from the citrus grove,
Where fruit shoots confetti and critters all rove.
A small orange snail leads the parade,
While fireflies join in, all light and unafraid.

With a squirt of zest, the trees tell a joke,
While chipmunks crack up, oh what a poke!
The world seems to sparkle, laughing away,
In a twilight waltz of the citrus ballet!

Swaying in the Citrus Haze

In a garden where the sun sings,
Buzzing bees do silly things.
Wobbling on their tiny feet,
Dancing round to a fruity beat.

Lemonade dreams float on the breeze,
Tickling noses, such a tease.
A jester's hat upon the tree,
Laughing leaves, wild and free.

Squirrels plot their fruity heist,
Planning mischief, oh so nice.
With a wink and cheeky grin,
Round and round, where to begin?

Bright yellow frolic, oh what fun!
Citrus magic, second to none.
In this playground of zest and cheer,
Joy abounds throughout the year.

Golden Hues of Afternoon

In the sunlight, shadows play,
Fruit flies joining in the fray.
Chasing rays, they flit and sway,
In a dance that's here to stay.

Panic hits when they collide,
Buzzing buddies full of pride.
Over ripe fruits they conspire,
Wobbling like they're on a wire.

Sipping nectar, what a scene,
Nature's pranks, oh how they glean.
Lemons laughing at the plan,
Even fruit flies join the jam.

Golden rays, a giggle fest,
Who knew fruits could jest so best?
In this garden, luck is sweet,
A comedy of sun and heat.

Beyond the Blossoms, a Soft Sigh

In the orchard, sweet scents bloom,
Giggling trees dispel the gloom.
Branches bow from laughs they share,
Even bark has jokes to spare.

Red squirrels launch a mighty leap,
While lazy bees take all their sleep.
In the shade of a citrus swell,
Chuckleberries start to yell.

Pips and pits, a playful game,
Citrus sweet, but who's to blame?
Witty critters with a jest,
Spoiling fruit, they find it best.

Underneath the laughing skies,
Nature's pranks can be quite wise.
In this scene of fruity bliss,
Who could ever seal the kiss?

A Breeze Through Sun-Kissed Orchards

A gentle breeze begins to tease,
Poking sticks at buzzing bees.
Giggling flowers sway in glee,
What a fruit-filled jubilee!

Tailored tricks from critters small,
Nature's laughter fills the hall.
Wiggling stems and tails that twirl,
Sunshine plays in a citrus whirl.

Chickens dance in a feathered spree,
Frogs join in, oh can't you see?
Every petal's got a tale,
In this orchard, fun won't fail.

A carousel of colors bright,
Emerald leaves and golden light.
In this garden, joy's the plot,
Making merriment, or not!

A Brighter Future in Petal's Promise

In gardens where the sunbeams play,
A sneaky bee just flew away.
With pollen stuck all on his back,
He thinks he's got a little snack.

The breeze delivers citrus cheer,
As butterflies come fluttering near.
They giggle as they swirl and spin,
In petal skirts, they've found their kin.

Oh, gingerly the ants parade,
With tiny legs, they dance and wade.
Each one with dreams of sweet delight,
A conga line till the moon takes flight.

A squirt of juice, a zesty grin,
The fruit flies laugh, they dive right in.
With giggles echoing all around,
They crown the garden, joy unbound!

The Allure of Unseen Delights

Between the leaves, a mischief stirs,
A squirrel dons his little furs.
He spots a fruit, a hefty prize,
And winks at us with beady eyes.

A neighbor's cat pounces so sly,
As scented whispers float nearby.
He leaps, he bounds, but what a chase!
He trips and lands, oh what a face!

With every gust, the laughter flows,
A garden party no one knows.
The hedgehog winks with knowing glee,
As all unite to make a spree.

So raise a glass of fragrant zest,
To all the friends who know what's best!
The strange delights that make us smirk,
In nature's jest, we find our quirks!

Citrus Spheres Above the Ground

Up high they bob, those sunny spheres,
Each round and bright, ignites our cheers.
They sway and swing from branches fine,
Chasing dreams of juice and wine.

Beneath, the critters scheme and plot,
A battle rages for the spot.
The snails glide slow with silly grins,
While birds dive down with clownish spins.

A fruit falls down, a comic thud,
As all the ants commence their flood.
They form a train, a sugary ride,
While giggles form on every side.

The sweetness lingers in the breeze,
As laughter echoes through the trees.
With every drop of zesty charm,
We find delights without alarm!

Harmony of Petals and Sky

The petals toss, they whirl and dance,
In tandem with a breezy chance.
A dandelion joins the fray,
And spins around in bright ballet.

A frog leaps by, a comical sight,
With jumps that make the world feel light.
He croaks a tune, off-key, yet proud,
His chorus met with laughter loud.

The sunbeams tickle every leaf,
As all partake in sheer relief.
With echoes of mirth in the air,
Humor blooms without a care.

So let us share a giggling spree,
In harmony, wild and free.
With nature's joke, we laugh and sway,
In this bright world, come join the play!

Songs of Sunshine and Blossom

Sunshine dances on the grass,
A squirrel prances, what a sass!
Bees wearing tiny sombreros,
Buzzing tunes like little heroes.

A bumblebee spilled all its drink,
On a flower, it gave a wink.
Laughing petals in bright parade,
Who knew flowers could be this swayed?

Butterflies in rainbow suits,
Doing cha-chas, oh what hoots!
As blooms giggle, spread their cheer,
Springtime antics bring us near.

In this garden, laughter brews,
Silly moments, nothing to lose.
Join the fun, don't let it fade,
Mysteries in petals laid.

Petals Unfurling in the Breeze

A flower's pirouette on stage,
Twirling slowly, like a mage.
A ladybug with shades so bright,
Dancing wildly, oh what a sight!

Petals whisper tales so funny,
Of sunshine, laughter, oh so sunny!
With a wink, they shake and sway,
Who knew blooms could have such play?

Daffodils, in yellow gowns,
Sway and giggle, upside-downs.
Their secrets spill with every breeze,
Tickling noses, with such ease!

So in this garden, life unfolds,
With every smile, joy never molds.
Join the revelry, feel the cheer,
Nature's party, the best time of year!

The Color of Sweetened Moments

In the orchard, fruits parade,
Dressed up well, they won't evade.
Giggling apples, grapes that tease,
Sharing tales with buzzing bees.

Citrus giggles fill the air,
Lemon-heads with quite the flair!
Tart and sweet, they twist and spin,
Right in the game, let's begin!

Plump oranges strut with flair,
Squeezed-out juice, without a care.
They burst in laughter, peel and all,
Rolling down, taking a fall!

Moments sweet as honey drips,
Leaves us laughing, joyful quips.
With every taste, a smile blooms,
In this garden, joy resumes!

Citrus Muse in Springtime's Glow

Under clouds of cotton candy,
Citrus dreams are oh so dandy.
Jokes on trees, as branches sway,
Tickling fruit, in fun display.

Orange peels, a playful glide,
On breezes soft, they take a ride.
Tarts and sweets in crazy mix,
Nature's laughter, here's the fix!

While sipping nectar with the bees,
We share whispers in the breeze.
Fruits wearing crowns, a royal jest,
Tickle your taste buds with the best!

So gather round, let laughter soar,
In here, springtime will restore.
Join the fun, let spirits lift,
Nature's bounty is a gift!

Citrus Serenade in Gentle Winds

In the garden, giggles bloom,
Trees swaying to their own tune.
Buzzing bees wear tiny hats,
Dancing near the playful rats.

Sunlight spills like lemonade,
On the blooms, a grand parade.
The flowers wear their sunny smiles,
While squirrels scamper in wild styles.

Fluttering wings of yellow hue,
As squirrels sing a song or two.
The air tickles with laughter's grace,
As butterflies begin their race.

With juiced-up jokes and zestful cheer,
The garden plays, come join the sphere!
So grab your hat and come on out,
In this madness, there's no doubt!

Sun-Kissed Ambrosia

A tasty sunbeam takes a bow,
As bushes grin, 'Beware of cow!'
Juicy giggles spill from trees,
While ants line up like movie fees.

The citrus tickles with a zing,
While chubby bunnies hop and sing.
In this orchard, fun's the rule,
As birds make jokes while taking a stool.

Squirrels wear their finest threads,
Sipping nectar from flower beds.
A burlesque dance of buzzing bees,
In pursuit of nectar, oh, what tease!

So join the feast, it's quite absurd,
Where laughter flies, and jokes are stirred.
Life's a carnival, a joyful quest,
In this sun-drenched, citrus fest!

Blossoms of Brightest Yellow

A parade of petals, oh what fun,
With dancing stripes and pranks begun.
The wind joins in with a silly cheer,
As bees debauch on sweet root beer.

Cartwheeling bugs in tights so bright,
While ladybugs spin with all their might.
The pollen flows like laughter's stream,
And each small critter lives the dream.

A tree in bloom dons a party dress,
While squirrels hold a juggling contest.
Chasing shadows in a sunny jam,
Who knew veggies could become a ham?

With fruity puns and zest-filled cheers,
This garden giggles through all its years.
So take a seat, join this crazy ride,
Where joy and fruitfulness collide!

Whispering Pollen Trails

In the air, a buzz of delight,
With pollen jokes flying in flight.
The blossoms waltz like hippos in shoes,
While grasshoppers share their best news.

Glorious scents of zestful glee,
Wobbling worms invite you to see.
The flowers chit-chat and spill the tea,
Be careful, though, it might tickle thee!

Tiny dung beetles as dance crew,
Spinning tales of pollen like dew.
Carrying laughter with every roll,
In this garden, there's joy in the stroll.

So tread softly on this fragrant trail,
Where laughter dances and stories prevail.
This whimsical air, so wild and grand,
Come grab a friend and lend them a hand!

The Elixir of Spring's Warm Embrace

A cheeky breeze whispers loud,
Tickling bees, they dance in a crowd.
Citrus giggles on the sunny street,
As squirrels sport their zesty feet.

A spider spun a sticky nest,
To catch the scent, oh what a quest!
A butterfly with a silly grin,
Tripped on petals, lost in a spin.

Chasing aromas high and low,
Finding sweetness in the show.
Citrus smiles, make spring so bright,
Even clouds feel light and polite.

Giggling daisies, wild and free,
Join the fun, come dance with me.
With every sip of sunlight's glee,
We toast to joy and citrus tea!

Citrus Magic in the Afternoon

Orange puns float with the breeze,
Lemon jokes that tickle the knees.
A sunbeam juggles with its light,
And butterflies take off in flight.

The trees wear hats of vibrant hue,
While bumblebees sing a giggly tune.
Oh, to sip from a zest-filled cup,
Where the laughter spills and helps us up.

A frolicsome breeze, cheeky and bold,
Brings tales of warmth the sun has told.
Even the ants wear little smiles,
As they strut their things in sunny styles.

With each bright sprout, we leap and twirl,
A zany dance, a happy whirl.
In the afternoon, joy takes the stage,
Where citrus laughs are all the rage!

Parfums of the Orchard Wind

Whiffs of fun drift through the trees,
As playful gusts do as they please.
The fruits wear hats made of a grin,
And sprinkle joy upon our skin.

Each blossom laughs, a tickle here,
The pollen flirts, oh dear oh dear!
With every gust, there's endless cheer,
And silly antics that draw us near.

The orchard swings on laughter's vine,
Where citrus jokes taste just divine.
A dance of color, oh what a thrill,
As breezes play at their own sweet will.

With buzzing friends all around,
In golden hues, delight is found.
The orchard winds with silly flair,
Bring out the giggles in the air!

Sweet Songs from Golden Petals

Golden petals, oh what a sight,
Sway and wiggle with sheer delight.
A butterfly dances, sets the stage,
While blossoms giggle, turn the page.

Bees in sunglasses zip and weave,
Carrying joy, it's hard to believe!
Every bloom sings a funky tune,
Even the trees sway to the moon.

Breezes tickle with fragrant hands,
Whispering secrets that nature plans.
Laughter sprinkles like morning dew,
As flowers share tales, old yet new.

In this whacky, zesty affair,
Joy spills out without a care.
So come, join the flower parade,
With sweet songs, let worries fade!

Sunlight and Floral Harmony

The sun plays hide and seek,
While blooms start to giggle,
They dance on whispers bright,
In a citrusy wiggle.

A bee with shades so cool,
Buzzes in perfect time,
He drinks the juice of joy,
And adds a twist to rhyme.

With fragrant laughs around,
The garden is a stage,
Where scents and smiles collide,
Each petal turns a page.

Oh, nature's cheeky show,
With colors so alive,
Sunlight and blooms collide,
In a jolly, sweet high five!

A Tapestry of Citrus Scent

In a quilt of sunny zest,
Laughter fills the day,
As petals weave and swirl,
Chasing clouds away.

A squirrel with a grin,
Jumps high to steal the show,
While blossoms trade their jokes,
In a crafty little row.

The breeze tosses confetti,
Of citrus and delight,
And every leaf that flutters,
Wins a giggle, so light.

With scents that tickle noses,
And smiles that chase all frowns,
This tapestry of fun,
Turns all the world around!

Petals Softly Falling

The petals take a tumble,
Like stars that fell from space,
They giggle on the ground,
In a messy, joyful race.

A dog spins in the sun,
Chasing scents like a pro,
While bees start belly laughing,
In this sweet citrus show.

Raindrops dance with hijinks,
On leaves with a splashy cheer,
And nature's grand performance,
Brings giggles far and near.

When petals softly tumble,
And laughter fills the air,
Life's a sunny party,
With those sweet scents everywhere!

Butterflies and Citrus Dreams

Butterflies wear their best,
In colors bright and bold,
They flutter past their friends,
With stories yet untold.

A caterpillar jokes,
On a leaf that's quite absurd,
"I'll race you to the bloom,"
Is the funniest word heard!

The sun winks down below,
As laughter starts to sway,
While dreams of zestful light,
Turn ordinary to play.

Wings brushing past the scent,
Of joys both sweet and rare,
Butterflies spread laughter,
In a cheerful, bright affair!

Sweet Citrus Dreams Take Flight

A zesty thought floats by,
With giggles chasing bees,
A lemon thought, oh my,
In a world of fragrant breeze.

Dancing round the fruit tree,
With a twist and a laugh,
Making lemonade glee,
In my citrus-themed staff.

Jumpsuits made of yellow,
Sipping drinks with a straw,
Feeling bright and quite mellow,
Oh, what a fruity law!

Sweet dreams take to the sky,
Like bubbles made of cheer,
A citrus flight, oh my!
Let laughter rule the year.

Garden's Breath of Sunshine

In the garden, oh so bright,
Critters giggle in delight,
A sunflower takes its flight,
Making all the flowers tight.

Bumblebees in silly dance,
Wobbling with a funny glance,
Spreading joy in their prance,
While the daisies take a chance.

The sun spills laughter wide,
With petals all around,
In this place, fun won't hide,
Where nature's joy is found.

A cabbage rolls with glee,
And carrots giggle too,
In this garden jubilee,
Everything's bright and new.

The Harmonies of Golden Light

A symphony of citrus notes,
With laughs that dance and play,
In the air, the laughter floats,
Chasing clouds away.

Harmonies from trees so tall,
Whisper soft and sweet,
Crickets join the lively call,
With rhythm in their feet.

Glow of gold beneath the blue,
Nature's jesters in a line,
Every moment feels brand new,
Sipping sunshine, oh so fine.

As the day turns into night,
Twinkling stars appear and wink,
The world bursts with pure delight,
In the citrus link we think.

Petals Painting the Sky

With a flick, the petals fly,
Painting scenes of joy and cheer,
Each one dreams to touch the sky,
With colors bold and clear.

A whirlwind of yellow and green,
Sprinkling laughter on the ground,
The silliest sights ever seen,
A happy dance all around.

Breezes brush with gentle hands,
Waltzing with the dandelions,
In this world where joy expands,
And laughter becomes the ions.

So let's twirl and skip away,
In this vibrant, funny game,
Where petals paint a bright ballet,
And nothing is ever the same.

Scents of a Golden Reverie

In a garden full of glee,
The bees hum with such esprit.
They dance on petals, light and quick,
As I attempt a honey trick.

The squirrels ponder, tails held high,
While I watch them with a sigh.
Their antics funny, a comic show,
Nature's jesters steal the glow.

My shoes are sticky, what a plight!
A lemon pie? I think I might.
But first, I'll chase a butterfly,
Oops! There it goes, oh my oh my!

A fragrant dream, a zesty blend,
With laughs and joy, I will transcend.
In this orchard, life feels so sweet,
Let's twirl and dance on joyful feet.

Citrus Blossoms Among the Hives

The bees have gathered quite a buzz,
They flirt with blooms as they should,
One winked at me, what a bold move!
I waved back, not sure what to prove.

A ladybug wears sunglasses bright,
Strutting 'round, what a funny sight!
With tiny swagger, it takes the stage,
Stealing the show at this leaf-green page.

A cat pranced through, with style so grand,
Wearing a flower crown, quite unplanned.
It batted at petals, with such grace,
Oh, how I wish I could keep pace!

The air is sweet, a comical tune,
While I dance under dusky moon.
All creatures sing a joyful song,
In citrus fields, where we belong.

An Orchard's Heartbeat of Colors

In the orchard where colors collide,
The fruits wave their arms, full of pride.
A rogue squirrel steals the brightest hue,
With a chuckle, I'm feeling blue.

A parrot on a branch does cheer,
Squawking jokes, oh dear, oh dear!
The oranges snicker, peeking from leaves,
As pranks unfold, the laughter weaves.

With floppy hats made of twigs and grass,
We'll fashion crowns, let the mem'ry pass.
But then I trip on a twist of vine,
As flowers giggle, oh, I feel divine!

Nature's palette, wild and bright,
Paints my heart with pure delight.
Amidst this whimsy, let's rejoice,
In silly antics, let laughter voice.

The Breath of Golden Sunsets

As daylight fades, a funny sight,
The fireflies flicker with bright delight.
They tease the shadows, blushing red,
While families of rabbits hop in bed.

A sunflower nods its head with zest,
As the crickets play their twilight fest.
With a twist and flop, they break into dance,
Their chirps in rhythm make hearts prance!

The breeze carries whispers of jokes untold,
While I nibble snacks that are oh-so-gold.
A chipmunk pokes its head for a nib,
And suddenly, we're all in a rib!

The sunset laughs, a warm embrace,
Sprinkling fun at an endless pace.
In this moment, let joy spread far,
As nature winks, a brilliant star.

Hints of Gold on Gentle Breezes

Whiffs of yellow float on by,
As bees parade beneath the sky.
A citrus giggle in the sun,
Who knew fruit could be so fun?

Trees wear smiles with zestful grace,
While critters join this vibrant race.
Squirrels stash their snacks with flair,
As laughter mingles in the air.

The dandelions twirl in cheer,
Echoing the joy that's near.
Chasing shadows with whimsy bold,
Life's a joke that's yet untold.

And in this sunshine, all is bright,
As friends get lost in pure delight.
When life throws slices, take a bite,
For fun is always within sight.

The Sweetness of Citrus Days

On sunny days, the world's aglow,
With laughter dancing to and fro.
The orange peels roll down the lane,
A game of tag, who will win fame?

A picnic spread, all citrus neat,
Where ants conspire to take a seat.
They plan a feast, so sly, so quick,
But all they get is a citrus trick!

The puddles splash with tangy glee,
Our shirts stained bright with zestful spree.
We toast with cups of sunny cheer,
And giggle loud, for spring is here!

So let us sip on lemonade,
With silly straws, our plans we've made.
In sun-kissed moments, we shall play,
And cherish every citrus day.

Fluttering from Orchard to Sky

Colors swirl with cheeky flair,
As breezes tickle every hair.
With petals flapping like a flag,
They wave hello and tease the snag.

A butterfly sports a citrus grin,
While squirrels plot their next wild win.
The oranges giggle from the tree,
As that rascally wind sets them free!

With each tumble, a raucous sound,
Nature salsa on the ground.
And birds chirp jokes of tangy treats,
While critters dance in fancy feats.

So fling your worries to the sky,
With a zestful twirl and a playful sigh.
For every twist and every spin,
Brings laughter where the fun begins.

Aura of Spring's Golden Glow

Yellow hues paint the joyful scene,
As nature's cheer takes center screen.
Bumblebees hum a silly tune,
While flowers giggle, blooming soon!

The sunlight sprinkles, a golden dust,
Creating smiles, it's an absolute must.
We gather round with grins so wide,
As giggles soar, we take our stride.

In the orchard, mischief sings,
Nature's playground, oh, the things!
With citrus laughs and playful grins,
Each day begins where joy has wins.

So come and join in this warm glow,
Where everyone is free to show.
For joy is ripe, let's raise a cheer,
In spring's soft arms, we disappear.

Sun-Drenched Aromas of New Beginnings

In a garden where zest appears,
Silly bees dance, full of cheers.
They wear tiny hats, bright and gold,
Sipping nectar, feeling bold.

The sun winks down, a golden eye,
While butterflies twirl, oh my, oh my!
Spraying joy in the afternoon,
Nature's own merry cartoon.

Tiny fruits tease from branches high,
With citrus giggles, they pass by.
Expectant scents beckon us near,
To frolic and laugh, with no fear.

Daydreams burst like a citrus pop,
In a world where the giggles won't stop.
So let's dance where the flavors mix,
In sunshine's warm and zesty fix.

Whispers of Citrus and Sunshine

A cheeky breeze sprinkles delight,
As squirrels play dress-up, a funny sight.
Their tails like ribbons, fluffing the air,
With citrus scent hiding everywhere.

The laughter of leaves as they shimmy,
Reminds us of joy, soft and zippy.
Squirrels bark jokes, striking a pose,
Under the arches where sunshine glows.

The fruit hangs low, a tempting tease,
Watch out! Buzzed bees, if you please!
They buzz with jokes, oh what a trip,
Offering smiles with each little sip.

From fragrant blooms bursts raucous fun,
Nature's jesters, we've just begun!
So let's chase the giggles today,
In this bright dance that won't fade away.

Bright Petals, Soft Whispers

Petals open, saying hello,
Winking at sunshine, putting on a show.
With sprightly hues, they flitter and play,
Like kids in a field on a sun-soaked day.

They whisper secrets of laughter and joy,
While butterflies zoom like a child's toy.
Swirling and twirling in sweet harmony,
In a circus of blooms, wild and free.

The air is tickled with zestful cheer,
As bees spin tales as they buzz near.
With each tiny drop, a giggle escapes,
Like nature crafted playful japes.

In this bouquet of sunshine's embrace,
Life takes a moment to slow down the pace.
So come join the fun, let worries cease,
As bright petals bob in a dance of peace.

Nature's Yellow Symphony

In the garden's vibrant stage,
Nature laughs, it's all the rage.
A concerto of fruit, sweet and bright,
Bumbles and chirps are pure delight.

Harmony echoes in every breeze,
While ants march like a band of keys.
They tap and stomp in rhythm divine,
Creating a shuffle, oh so fine!

The zesty giggle of aromatic life,
Makes even the grumpiest critters rife.
Fluffy clouds drift, taking a peek,
To join in the fun, it's playful and cheek.

With smiles all round, and no signs of gloom,
Joyful echoes in brightly lit bloom.
So let's be merry, let's sing along,
In Nature's symphony, where we belong.

The Poetry of Bright Hues

In the garden where humor stews,
Sunshine sparkles, dancing views.
Bees in bow ties, buzzing glee,
Tickling petals, what a spree!

Daffodils wear shades of cheer,
While squirrels jot jokes, oh dear!
Crickets chirp a playful song,
As if they know they don't belong!

From petals puffs of laughter rise,
Butterflies donning fancy ties.
A party hosted by the breeze,
Attracting giggles from the trees!

So join the fun, no need to stare,
In floral realms, grin with flair.
When whimsy colors every scene,
We toast to life and all its green!

Zesty Enchantment in the Air

Sprightly flavors fill the day,
As fruits in wigs come out to play.
Bananas slip, giggles ensue,
Tangerines in a merry queue!

Jesters of the garden stand,
With peels like crowns, they take command.
Citrus clowns with playful tricks,
Sprinkle laughter like magic pix!

Grapefruits juggling on their sides,
As lemon fairies ride the tides.
They twirl and twist in vibrant hue,
Sending smiles to all in view!

With zest for fun, the air is bright,
Every corner ignites with light.
So come and bask in laughter's glow,
Where citrus dreams put on their show!

Breaths of Spring's Awakening

Springtime giggles start to sprout,
From every nook, a cheerful shout.
The blooms awake with silly grace,
Juicy jokes all over the place!

Dewdrops wearing party hats,
Chasing butterflies, silly brats.
They feast on humor, light and free,
In nature's grand comedy!

Tulips tease with blush and wink,
While dandelions plot and think.
With whispers that tickle the breeze,
And laughter shared among the trees!

As spring unfolds her quirky ways,
Each petal sings in merry plays.
Join the laughter, dance and prance,
In the joy of blooms, there's a chance!

Citrus Nectar's Serenade

In the orchard, mischief brews,
Sweet and tart in vibrant hues.
With every sip, a chuckle flows,
From citrus cups, the humor grows!

A tangerine sings a funny tune,
Juggling seeds beneath the moon.
Orange peels flip with delight,
Engaging critters in their flight!

Grapefruit giggles in the sun,
Souring woes, oh what fun!
Pineapple dons a crown so grand,
Drawing chuckles across the land!

So lift your glass to nature's jest,
With nectar sweet, we're truly blessed.
In every drop, a world to share,
With laughter swirling through the air!

The Aroma of Sun-drenched Mornings

In gardens where bees buzz and dart,
The fruit jokes ripen, playing their part.
A sneeze, a sniff—a citrus parade,
Fruit-faces dance, unafraid of their shade.

The sun's warm grin, a vitamin spree,
Citrus cereal? What a sight to see!
Oranges prance down the breakfast line,
While grapefruits giggle, feeling just fine.

With zest and zeal they join the fun,
Wearing tiny hats, a fruity pun.
They take to the stage, forget the grind,
Start a comedy act, all fruit, no rind.

So toss those peels, let laughter swell,
In the orchard, where the fruits rebel.
Squeeze some joy, let go of despair,
In this citrus circus, all is rare!

Citrus Elation in the Crafted Garden

In a garden where the sun does play,
Fruits wear costumes in a zany display.
The limes wear glasses, the lemons dance,
Tomatoes join in with a silly prance.

The mint feels fresh, in a minty fight,
While oranges juggle in morning light.
Lemonade pools, a splash, a surprise,
As grapefruits toss laughs behind their eyes.

Each plant a character, a role to portray,
With citrus wit, they bring joy each day.
Fans wave leaves, as oranges take a bow,
In this crafted haven, they're funny somehow.

So come take a peek, don't be shy,
In this garden of giggles, let laughter fly.
With every bite, a chuckle to share,
In the crispy zest, humor fills the air.

In the Heart of Citrus Fantasies

In the heart of dreams where fruits absurd,
Lemons sing songs, cheeky and heard.
With each little breeze, they crack up the sky,
While oranges plot a fruity pie.

A lemon once thought he could wear a hat,
But fell off a branch—splat! Just like that.
Bananas giggle, the avocados rhyme,
Creating a rhythm, a fruity prime.

They roll and they tumble, making a scene,
Grapefruits announcing—what's funny but mean?
Yet they all break into laughter so bright,
Under the sun, everything feels right.

So join in the fun, let your worries cease,
In this citrus world, find joy and peace.
As laughter erupts from this fruity spree,
Even the seeds share a chuckle with me!

Aromatic Affections Under Sunshine

Under a sunbeam, the orangey crew,
Bakes in the warmth, making moments anew.
With zesty high-fives, they roll in the grass,
Where laughter erupts, and time seems to pass.

The lemons wear sunglasses, so cool and bright,
Trading silly jokes till the far end of night.
The limes tease the lemons, a playful spat,
While berries giggle in their fruity chat.

A picnic is set, with drinks full and bright,
They toast to the day, a real citrus fright.
With every sip, a chuckle erupts,
In this sun-kissed gathering, joy is corrupt.

So raise a glass, let laughter spill wide,
Join in the fun on this citrus ride.
In this sweet sun-soaked laughter affair,
Aromatic moments float light in the air.

When Yellow Meets the Wind

A breeze, it brings a twisty tale,
Of yellow winks and scents that sail.
Embrace the laughter, skip the gloom,
Nature's jesters bloom in rooms.

The fruits, they giggle high and low,
As petals twirl in zippy flow.
Bouncing past with chuckles bright,
A fruity jest in morning light.

With every puff, a twang of zest,
Playful whispers, nature's jest.
The neighbors laugh, they join the fun,
In gardens where the jokes are spun.

A sunny day with trickster flair,
Leaves wiggle in the fragrant air.
So grab your hats and join the game,
Where yellow dreams are never tame.

Whispered Secrets of the Grove

In secret nooks, where giggles grow,
The fruity laughter starts to show.
A yellow wink, a breezy tease,
Where cheeky blooms dance with the bees.

Each petal's tale is full of glee,
As roots conspire beneath the tree.
The critters prance with sly delight,
In sunshine's glow, what a sight!

Whispers echo through the leaves,
Funny jests that no one believes.
A budding romance with every bloom,
As joy spills out, a bright perfume.

So if you wander where it's sweet,
Join in the laughs, skip on your feet.
In joyful groves, where secrets blend,
The fun continues, never ends.

Citrus-Scented Memories at Dusk

As dusk descends, the laughter grows,
Fruity faces in sunset's glow.
The evening air hums songs of cheer,
Silly dances, come join the sphere!

Ticklish breezes play around,
In citrus dreams, where joy is found.
Fruity jokes hang in the sky,
With every giggle, a playful sigh.

Old memories twist like vines entwined,
A carousel of jokes, refined.
With every swirl, a punchline flies,
In this sweet realm, all laughter tries.

So as night falls, the fun ignites,
With zestful whispers, joyous flights.
In citrus realms, we'll always stay,
As twilight brings more games to play.

Dance of Fragrance and Light

In the light of day, a dance begins,
With giggles bursting from nature's sins.
Yellow petals shimmy and sway,
As laughter joins this bright ballet.

The fragrance floats on wobbly tunes,
Where tree-top jokers hide like loons.
Each step a twirl, each spin a jest,
In the warm sun, we feel our best.

As shadows play and smiles ignite,
The wings of joy take daring flight.
With every bloom, we crack a grin,
In the fragrant waltz, we all win.

So come and join this merry spree,
Let yellow hues set your heart free.
In the final bow, we pause to cheer,
For fragrances and laughter, dear!

Citrus Whispering Dreams

In the orchard, whispers play,
Fruity tales in bright arrays.
One cheeky fruit, full of glee,
Says, "I'm zestier than thee!"

Flavors dance on breezy trails,
Tickled tongues and citrus tales.
Juicy jokes in every bite,
Sour giggles, pure delight!

Lemon drops from trees above,
Laughing like a shady dove.
"Why so serious?" they tease,
"Life is better with some squeeze!"

In this grove, mischief brews,
Scented laughter, lemon hues.
Join the fruit, let voices rise,
In this garden, joy defies!

Fragrance of Sunlit Gardens

Underneath the golden rays,
Scented jokes weave through the maze.
Flowers giggle, petals play,
"Who smells sweeter? Hip or sway?"

Gardens hum a citrus tune,
Bouncing tunes from noon to moon.
Every fruit has got a quirk,
"Try my juice, it's quite the perk!"

Bees are buzzing, wearing hats,
Dancing 'round like chubby brats.
"Oh, what fun!" they laugh and hum,
"Catch us if you can, you scrum!"

In this sunny, fragrant spree,
Nature's laughter sets us free.
Silly moments fill the air,
Joy is found everywhere!

Zest of Spring's Embrace

Spring arrives with bubbly vibes,
Citrus laughter, funny jibes.
Tiny blooms all laugh and sway,
Silly fruit join in the play!

"Who can squeeze the most today?"
One bold orange yells, "Okay!"
Fruits embark on playful fights,
Zesty giggles light the nights!

Calls of citrus, wild and bright,
Sparkling tales in morning light.
Chasing lemons, oh what fun!
Each a jester, all should run!

Silly scents on breezes sweep,
Fragrant dreams that never sleep.
With each bloom, we sing and dance,
Embracing spring as if in trance!

Golden Petals on a Breeze

Petals flutter, soft and light,
A citrus dance, a pure delight.
Laughing flowers, cheeky and bold,
Tell the secrets they behold!

On the breeze, a fragrant chase,
Peeling laughter, silly grace.
"Catch the scent, it's lemony!"
"Not so fast! I've got to flee!"

Fruits in dresses, oh what sights,
Dancing wildly, sweet delights.
"Who's the funniest?" one cries out,
"Every fruit!" they all shout out!

Golden petals, swirling free,
Spread their joy for all to see.
In this garden, smiles appear,
Funny fruits bring endless cheer!

Golden Hues of Springtime

Golden rays begin to beam,
A fairy dance, or so it seems.
Buzzing bees in tiny hats,
Stealing nectar from the mats.

Birds wear coats of vibrant cheer,
Chirping jokes for all to hear.
With every bloom, a loud applause,
Where frolic leads to funny flaws.

Squirrels grin with puffy cheeks,
As they pretend to play hide and seek.
The flowers giggle, bright and bold,
In sunlight's arms, they spin and fold.

Springtime's antics, never tame,
Nature's jesters play the game.
With laughter ringing through the trees,
It seems the season's here to tease.

Through the Canopy of Citrus

Beneath the trees with fruity crowns,
The laughter dances all around.
A lemon says, 'I'm feeling fine!'
While orange jokes on the nearby vine.

The lime is zesty, full of glee,
His jokes are sour — wait and see!
The air is filled with citrus puns,
A fruity fest for everyone.

A clever sprout, wearing a hat,
Teases a bee — 'You're way too fat!'
The flowers nod, they just can't wait,
To roll on laughter, isn't it great?

Through the branches, giggles sprout,
Each breeze whispers, 'Dare not pout!'
The canopy holds joyful sights,
As day drifts into citrus nights.

Dance of the Zesty Flowers

In gardens bright, a jolly show,
With petals pink and yellow glow.
They sway and twirl, the breeze their host,
These zesty blossoms love to boast.

A daisy shouts, 'Come join the fun!'
While tulips giggle, 'We've just begun!'
The roses sigh, 'Oh, we're so grand!'
As daisies leap, a hand in hand.

Here comes a daffodil with flair,
He trips and says, 'I'm in midair!'
The sun sends rays, a spotlight beam,
As flowers dance, fulfilling dreams.

A jester's rogue, they grow and sway,
In zesty hues, they laugh and play.
With each soft breeze, they take a chance,
In nature's world, they prance and dance.

A Symphony of Citrus Dreams

The orchestra of zesty scents,
Plays silly tunes that make no sense.
The conductor? A cheeky bee,
With tiny wings and grand esprit.

The trumpets blast with citrus cheer,
While lemons giggle, 'Can you hear?'
The violins — they softly hum,
To every rhythm, bees go bzz and drum.

With zestful beats, the flowers sway,
A concert bright, come join the fray!
The daisies clap, the pansies grin,
In citrus dreams, we all dive in.

As twilight falls, the show's not through,
The stars join in with laughter too.
In fragrant air, symphonies soar,
In this sweet world, we laugh for more.

Fragrance Gathering with the Breeze

A swarm of scents takes flight,
Like socks that skipped laundry night.
They bump and giggle through the trees,
Tickling noses in the summer's tease.

Bees dance awkward, in a rush,
While butterflies join in the hush.
They swirl and twirl, a silly sight,
As blossoms laugh in pure delight.

Each petal's blush, a comical tune,
As bees hum loudly, sounding like a loon.
So, catch the breeze—don't let it fade,
Sneeze and giggle in this fragrant parade!

With citrus cheer, they caper high,
As echoes of laughter fill the sky.
A funny show, nature's grand jest,
When scent and humor meet—oh, the best!

Citrus Kisses and Scented Whispers

A breeze so sweet, it kisses cheeks,
And whispers tales of fruity feats.
With zestful giggles, scents collide,
In this fragrant game, we all abide.

Squirrels wear hats made of peel,
Pretending grandness, oh, what a deal!
They prance about, a citrus rave,
While the ants hold hands, feeling brave.

In this comedic garden crew,
The bees outshine with quirky hue.
With air so dense, we can't resist,
A laugh, a grin, we coexist!

So grab a spritz, come join the jest,
In scented whispers, we are blessed.
With humor sweet as summer's birth,
Let's twirl and laugh, embracing mirth!

The Dance of Yellows Underneath the Sky

The sun beams down—a bright estate,
While flowers jiggle, it's quite the fate.
In yellow gear, they shake and sway,
Making mischief in a floral ballet.

With bees in tutus, and bugs in spats,
It's a riot, this garden of chitchat.
They whirl and twirl, no need for grace,
Stumbling through their happy place.

Laughter erupts, like petals stored,
In every nook where joy is poured.
A fruity rendezvous joins the fun,
As oddball aromas in the sun.

So dance along, let humor shine,
In the fruity festa, we intertwine.
A yellow riot, a fragrant spree,
Underneath this playful canopy!

Sweet Awakening Through Citrus Blooms

Awake, awake, the day in bloom,
With citrus giggles banishing gloom.
The air's a party—come take a share,
As zesty charms twirl everywhere.

A jester bee with polka-dot wings,
Buzzes along, sharing silly flings.
While flowers chuckle, their petals swirl,
In this fragrant world, watch laughter unfurl.

Sticky fingers from a fruity feast,
Dreams of lemonade—a summer beast!
With each burst of zest, a sparkling cheer,
Come laugh with us, the whimsy is here!

As blooms shower scents with playful delight,
Nature's jesters join in the fight.
For sweet awakenings that fill the air,
Let's dance together, without a care!

Citrus Seasons in Bloom

When life gives you tang, take a bite,
Just watch out for the pucker, it's quite a sight!
Oranges and lemons frolic and play,
In a zesty parade, they brighten the day.

Their yellow attire, a flamboyant show,
Dancing on trees, putting on a glow.
The squirrels join in with acorn hats,
While birds chirp tunes, and the world spins like that!

From morning to dusk, the laughter rings clear,
Sippin' on sunshine, that's the real cheer.
Tangy and sweet, a harmony bright,
In this citrus carnival, joy takes flight!

So raise up your glass, let's toast to the fun,
With citrusy giggles, we shine like the sun.
In this juicy realm where humor is king,
Every sip brings a smile; let the citrus bells ring!

A Promise of Sweetness

A grove full of hints, a secret so sly,
Where laughter is ripe, and mischief can fly.
With citrusy giggles hidden in trees,
Swirling like breezes, they know how to tease.

The fruit may seem quiet, in colors divine,
But they plot juicy jokes, oh what a design!
With every bright twist, they share a delight,
A chuckle, a wink, turning day into night.

Sunshine is sticky, like honey on toast,
As zesty giggles emerge, who could hate the most?
In this ticklish garden, humor blooms wide,
And we can't help but laugh with fruits as our guide!

So come for a taste, let's savor the cheer,
A promise of sweetness, let's toast with good beer.
In the world of the bright, with laughter our knack,
Every sip is a giggle, so let's not hold back!

Vibrant Aroma Rising Up

A scent in the air, oh what could it be?
Tickling your nose, it's a citrus jubilee!
With giggles infused in the golden delight,
The fruit's clever whispers, a socialite's night.

In this fragrant medley, jokes start to sprout,
The lemons conspire, what's this all about?
With zest on their lips, they play the jesters,
Bouncing with giggles, like fruity investors!

The oranges chuckle in their sunny attire,
As grapefruits waltz, dressed up to inspire.
No ordinary fruit, they hold the crown,
In a kingdom of laughter, where no one wears frown.

So let's take a stroll through this vibrant delight,
Where aromas of laughter can dance through the night.
In this world of citrus, let's twirl and prance,
For with every bright twist, we've got room to dance!

Garden of Golden Secrets

Step into a world where secrets unfold,
A garden of laughter, with stories retold.
Each fruit holds a joke, a curious tease,
While bees buzz about like they own the breeze.

Oh, the fruits whisper tales, with peels all aglow,
Drawing you close with a citrusy show.
The laughter's contagious, like pollen in flight,
As giggles escape in the soft evening light.

With tangy confessions and sweetness entwined,
In this wacky green paradise, joy you will find.
The oranges jest, while the limes roll their eyes,
In a whimsical world, where not one fruit lies!

So come pluck a smile from branches of cheer,
In this garden of secrets, there's no time for fear.
Each bite is a joke, every taste is a thrill,
In this field of delight, let's laugh and refill!

Flight of the Citrus Butterflies

In gardens bright where sunlight beams,
The zestful flyers flit in teams.
They tickle blooms with pollen darts,
And dance around with silly starts.

With wings like fruit in vibrant hues,
They sip on nectar, sassy snooze.
One trips and rolls, a clumsy flight,
Then lands headfirst, oh what a sight!

Their antics cause the flowers giggle,
As neighbors watch and give a wiggle.
"Oh dear!" they say, "What crazy fun!"
To see them flapping in the sun.

They buzz about, a citrus craze,
In happy mishaps, they all blaze.
With every flutter, laughter roars,
These air acrobats, we all adore!

Nature's Sunlit Brushstrokes

In fields where colors dance and play,
The painter's hand has gone astray.
With strokes of yellow, green, and zest,
A masterpiece of joy expressed.

The shrubbery is laughing loud,
While petals tangle in a crowd.
"Oh look!" they shout, "What a great mess!"
As colors swirl, they dance and dress.

A squirrel takes part, a tiny brush,
With every nibble, he brings a hush.
"I didn't sign up for this gig!"
But still he twirls, that cheeky twig!

In splashes bright, the world awakes,
With silly pranks that nature makes.
A canvas painted with pure glee,
In sunlit strokes, we long to be!

Essence of Joy in Petal Wings

With petals soft, a giggle floats,
On breezes light, like joyful notes.
They twirl and sway, a cheeky band,
In every wink, a ticklish hand.

"Oh dear me!" a flower sighs,
As butterflies dress up in ties.
They flaunt their colors, bold and bright,
Like party hats in pure delight.

A bumblebee comes by to see,
"Have you met my cousin, wee?"
The petals laugh, they share the cheer,
As pollen whispers, "Come on dear!"

In every flit, a secret shared,
A chuckle soft, the blooms all dared.
With petals swirling, joy takes flight,
In nature's fun, oh what a sight!

In the Heart of Citrusy Wings

In citrus realms where laughter thrives,
The silly wings make jolly dives.
One slips and slides on morning dew,
A bouncing act, oh what a view!

The flowers giggle, "What a show!"
As fluff and fluff do freely flow.
A butterfly busts out a dance,
While blossoms watch in joyful trance.

"Sign me up!" the daisies cheer,
"We want to join in all the fun here!"
With every flap, a stitch of mirth,
These fruity flyers own the earth.

In swirling hues, they paint the skies,
In citrus dreams, their laughter flies.
So come and join this merry spree,
Where petals laugh, and wild hearts free!

www.ingramcontent.com/pod-product-compliance
Lightning Source LLC
Chambersburg PA
CBHW070317120526
44590CB00017B/2711